Emma Sansom
Confederate Heroine

Margie Dover Ross

**Seacoast Publishing
Birmingham, Alabama**

Emma Sansom: Confederate Heroine

Published by Seacoast Publishing, Inc.
1149 Mountain Oaks Drive
Birmingham, Alabama 35226

Copyright © 2001 Margie Dover Ross

All rights reserved.
Reviewers and writers of magazine and newspaper articles are free to quote passages of this book as needed for their work. Otherwise, no part of this book may be reproduced or transmitted in any form or by any means, electronic or mechanical, including photocopying, recording or by any information storage and retrieval system, without the written permission of the publisher.

Library of Congress Card Number: 00-111458

Cover art by Thomas B. Moore

ISBN 1-878561-83-9

To obtain copies of this book, please write or call:
Seacoast Publishing, Inc.
Post Office Box 26492
Birmingham, Alabama 35260
(205) 979-2909

Dedication

For Mom and Dad,
Susan, Mark, Randall, Jeff and Jenny
...where all the stories really began.

To my family—my husband, Emmet and daughters Ashley and Allyson, who supported me all the way.
And to Maggie May for barking encouragement.

To librarians and historians everywhere—thank you for preserving our heritage.

To Confederates and Yankees who both fought valiantly in the Civil War and learned to live together peacefully when it was over. Thanks to their ancestors for preserving this rich heritage for future generations to study and learn from.

Finally to Tom Bailey, who brought a dream to reality.

Emma Sansom: Confederate Heroine

About The Series

Alabama Roots is a book series designed to provide reading pleasure for young people, to allow readers to better know the men and women who shaped the State of Alabama, and to fill a much-needed void of quality regional non-fiction for students in middle grades.

For years, teachers and librarians have searched for quality biographies about famous people from Alabama. This series is a response to that search. The series will cover a span of time from pre-statehood through the modern day.

The goal of *Alabama Roots* is to provide biographies that are historically accurate and as interesting as the characters whose lives they explore.

The *Alabama Roots* mark assures readers and educators of consistent quality in research, composition, and presentation.

The modern-day photographs in this book were taken by the author, Margie Dover Ross. Historical images are from photographs and drawings of the Civil War period.

Margie Dover Ross

Statue of Emma Sansom—pointing the way for General Nathan Bedford Forrest—stands atop monument to her and Forrest at the foot of a bridge across the Coosa River in Gadsden, Alabama.

Thundering Hooves

"BESSIE, SETTLE DOWN."

Even though she was mad, Emma Sansom coaxed the milk cow with her sweetest, softest voice. She knew it would do no good to be harsh with Bessie; it would only make the old cow more upset and fidgety.

Emma was frustrated with Bessie this morning. If her older brother Rufus was there, Bessie would be more cooperative.

But Rufus was gone. He signed up not long after the war started, and now he was who-knows-where fighting Yankees.

And that left the farm work for Emma and her older sister Jennie.

It was a late spring Alabama morning. The fields were wet from recent rains and as the sun climbed higher into the sky, it pulled a mist out of the damp earth. Things seemed so calm.

But Bessie wasn't. She was in no mood for milking. She stomped and moo-ed as if a bee was after her. Emma stroked Bessie's side. That always settled her down when Rufus did it.

"I don't know what is wrong with this cow," Emma groaned to Jennie. "She was always better for Rufus than me anyway."

"I miss Rufus," Emma went on. "I even miss Rufus when it's not milking time."

Jennie sighed in agreement and picked up a bucket that was leaning against the barn and walked slowly down to the well to get water, leaving Emma with her thoughts about Rufus and the troublesome milk cow.

Rufus could charm a barnyard. The animals always did just what he wanted them to do. It was almost like they were friends—Rufus and the animals.

Not for Emma. Especially not this morning. Bessie was worse than usual. She almost seemed nervous.

It was like Bessie knew something was about to happen. And it wasn't anything good.

"EMMA!"

Emma jerked her head up.

"EMMA!"

It was Jennie. She was racing back toward the

Emma Sansom: Confederate Heroine

barn, her bare feet hardly touching the ground.

"Horses!" Jennie gasped. "I heard horses.

"Lot-s-s-s of them."

The words spilled out even as Jennie gulped air to get her breath back.

"They're comin' f-f-fast."

Emma grabbed the milk stool and rushed to the fence. She tiptoed on the stool and peeked through the trees.

The roar of hooves was like thunder, but above the roar Emma could still hear her heart pounding she was so afraid and excited.

Suddenly, through the trees, she could see them coming.

Blue.

A flash of blue. Another. And another.

"It's Yankees," whispered Emma. "They are heading straight for our house."

It was the morning of May 2, 1863. The Civil War had found Emma Samsom. Her life was about to change forever.

Georgia

THIS IS THE STORY OF A COMMON FARM GIRL, a girl no different from thousands of others helping tend family farms during the Civil War.

But something special happened that day at her farm near Gadsden, Alabama; something so special that Emma Sansom would never be a common farm girl again.

Her story does not begin with the Yankees rushing up to her doorstep that May morning. It doesn't even begin in Alabama.

It begins in Social Circle, Georgia, a little village 165 miles east of Gadsden, Alabama. Emma was born there August 16, 1847. She was the twelfth and last child born to Micajah and Lamila Vann Sansom. She had six brothers and five sisters: Nancy Jane (called Jennie), Thomas, Ann, Martha, Eliza, William, John, Oren, Mary, James (called Joe) and Rufus. By the time

Emma Sansom: Confederate Heroine

Emma was born, some of her older brothers and sisters were married and starting families of their own.

Emma's parents were early settlers in Walton County, Georgia. Her father, Micajah Jr. was born in North Carolina and moved with his family to Social Circle, Georgia, in the early 1800s.

It was there that he met Lamila Vann.

In 1814, Micajah bought some land to farm in Jasper County, and on November 6, 1818 in Jasper County, Georgia, Micajah and Lamila were married.

Fifty miles east of where Atlanta is today, the land where Social Circle was founded was good farming country. When Micajah and Lamila moved there it was little more than a crossroads of two Creek Indian trails used for fur trading.

In just a few years more and more settlers moved in, carving farms out of the forest and planting fields. The trails got wider and wider until they turned into roads. Cabins and stores began to appear along the trail, and all of a sudden a whole village had developed.

It still did not have a name.

One day several of the farmers were sitting around the village well talking and drinking the cool well water when a stranger approached.

Margie Dover Ross

The villagers welcomed him with such warmth and friendliness that the stranger exclaimed, "This is surely a social circle."

The name stuck, and the village has been called Social Circle ever since. You can still find it on Georgia road maps today, just north of Interstate 20 on Highway 11.

This is where the Sansom family began and where Emma was born.

The farm was good to the Sansoms at first.

But it did not last.

They planted crops over and over on the same fields. Every year the crops were smaller and smaller. What was happening? They couldn't figure it out. No one knew that when a field is planted over and over, it wears the soil out so that there are no more nutrients to grow the crops.

When that happened, farmers began looking for new land. When his farm wore out, Emma's father looked west, to Alabama.

When the Sansom's first moved to Georgia, Alabama was a dark and mysterious land to the west. There were stories about hostile Creek Indians who had just lost a terrible war with America. Even though the Creeks had been beaten, there were reports of

Emma Sansom: Confederate Heroine

Creeks still raiding farms and killing the farmers.

There was good news about Alabama too. They were stories that made the Sansom's want to learn more about the land to the west—of cool, clear rivers and streams, of broad valleys where the land was so rich that plants just about jumped out of the ground.

Micajah and Lamila Sansom were not the only ones interested in those rich farmlands.

After the Creek Indian War, the soldiers from Andrew Jackson's Army went back home and talked about the wonderful land they had seen. The stories spread quickly north and east through Tennessee and Georgia into the Carolinas and Virginia.

Thousands of farmers wanted Alabama land.

Some came right on, even if it meant taking a chance with the Indians.

Others, like the Sansoms, held back.

In 1830, the United States Congress passed a law that changed things. The law was exciting to settlers who wanted to move into the new land west of Georgia.

It was a law that broke the hearts of thousands of Indians.

It was called the Indian Removal Act. It gave the President the power to move the Indians out of Alabama (and other parts of the Southeast) and send them to lands west of the Mississippi River, mostly in Oklahoma.

The Indians were rounded up and marched away. Many died on the trip.

It became known as The Trail of Tears.

With the Indians out of the way, settlers streamed into Alabama by the thousands.

Micajah Sansom was one of the cautious ones. He didn't just load up his family in a wagon and head out like some people did.

He left his wife and children in charge of the farm in Social Circle and went on a scouting trip to Alabama, to find just the right land for a new farm.

No one knows all the places he went.

But everyone knows where his search for new farmland ended.

The Coosa River flows from the northwest corner of Georgia into Alabama, and cuts across the state from northeast to southwest until it joins the Tallapoosa River just north of Montgomery to form the Alabama River.

In northeast Alabama, Lookout Mountain is just west of the river and for a distance runs more or less

Emma Sansom: Confederate Heroine

parallel to the river.

Just at the foot of the mountain lies one of the broadest, greenest valleys in all of northeast Alabama. Micajah knew it was the place.

He explored the area, and met the settlers who already had founded a little town nearby. The town was named Gadsden. They were friendly people, the kind that Micajah wanted to have for neighbors.

He rode the valley and found just the right place. Forty acres. It was good farmland, not a mile from where Lookout Mountain rises from the valley floor.

Right along their property flowed Black Creek. It would give them plenty of water for the animals. It wasn't the prettiest stream he had ever seen, but it was deep so he didn't have to worry about it drying up between rains.

Micajah went to the government offices in Cherokee County and registered the farm he had just bought. Once it had been Indian land, but the year was 1852, and the Indians had all been taken to Oklahoma several years earlier.

Micajah stayed and built the new farmhouse before going back to Social Circle for his family. The trip would be hard enough; he wanted them to have a place to live when they arrived.

Margie Dover Ross

Gadsden, Alabama

THE FAMILY KNEW that a move was coming, but it could not have meant much to little Emma.

In 1852 she was a five-year-old with lots of older brothers and sisters to tend to things. Some were already married and had families of their own.

It was an exciting time when Micajah gave them the news that he had bought a new farm and built a new home in Alabama.

Some of her older brothers and sisters who already were married were so excited about the area they decided to go there and buy land too. Others decided to stay in Georgia.

The Sansoms once had owned a slave named Aunt Fannie, but Micajah had given her her freedom.

But Aunt Fannie liked living with the Sansoms, and when they decided to move to Alabama, Aunt Fannie went with them.

Emma Sansom: Confederate Heroine

It was autumn when moving day finally arrived. The Sansoms loaded their belongings into wagons, said sad good-byes to their friends and children who were staying in Georgia, and climbed aboard for the long, bouncy dirt-road trip to Alabama.

There were stops along the way to rest, water and feed the animals, but for five-year-old Emma it was hard not to squirm and wonder how long the trip would take.

She was always ready to stop, get off the wagon and romp around long before Micajah was ready to stop to rest the animals.

She was just on a trip. There was no way for her or anyone else to know that she was riding to her place of destiny.

The sun sets early in Alabama in late October. And even though the sun still warms the days, the nights often turn chilly very quickly in north Alabama.

The light was beginning to fade when the Sansoms saw the cluster of homes and stores in the distance.

It was Gadsden, Alabama.

They were nearly home.

The townspeople recognized Micajah in an instant. He was the Georgia man who had just finished the new farmhouse on Black Creek. And here he was with his family, ready to move in.

"Welcome!" boomed a large voice.

"Hello, Micajah," said another enthusiastic voice, as folks began gathering around. "It's about time you brought all those young un's for us to meet."

Micajah smiled broadly. He was used to people teasing him about his large family. Micajah was proud of his wife and children. He began introducing them one-by-one, starting with his wife, Lamila.

Finally, he got to the end. "And last but certainly not least is Emma."

Emma looked up with radiant gray-blue eyes, and flashed a quick smile.

"Where is our new house?" she asked. She was ready to be home.

Her father looked down and laughed. "It is over by Black Creek, about two miles up the road. We're going to water the horses and mules and then we'll go to the new house," her father answered, smiling to himself at Emma's quick question.

Emma's father and brothers hitched the wagons to a post by the inn and began feeding and watering the mules.

Stagecoaches came and went, changing drivers

Emma Sansom: Confederate Heroine

and animals. The Inn was a busy place for the farm village. There was a general store close by, a blacksmith shop and a post office.

Next to the Inn was a grove of huge trees that spread out along the bluff. Over the bluff, the land fell away sharply to the slow-moving river below. It was the Coosa.

It was the river that got Gadsden going.

A steamboat captain named James Lafferty had come up river in the 1840s looking for a place to build a permanent landing. Gadsden was the spot he chose.

The settlers who were already in the area were so excited that Laffterty wanted to build a landing that they wanted to name the village Lafferty's Landing. But Captain Lafferty turned down the honor.

Instead, the settlers chose the name Gadsden in honor of Colonel James Gadsden who was famous for settling an important land dispute with Mexico at that time.

Just then, none of that mattered to little Emma. The cool dark of the autumn evening was gathering around her. Emma snuggled into her big sister's lap as they sat near the wagons. She was almost asleep.

Just then, a voice she knew so well made her jump. "Climb up, Emma, we're going to our new house by Black Creek," exclaimed her brother, Rufus.

Margie Dover Ross

He reached down and pulled her up on the wagon.

Everyone back in the wagons, Micajah reined the mules toward the road.

"Next and last stop, Black Creek."

Emma Sansom: Confederate Heroine

Black Creek

MICAJAH MIGHT HAVE BUILT A HOUSE, but there still was more than enough for everyone to do.

"You young un's come help us unload the wagons," Lamila called to everyone at the same time. "Rufus, you and the boys help your father tend to the animals and me and the girls will start settin' up the kitchen."

Then she started putting the house in order.

Micajah had done a good job building the house.

It was 66 feet wide and 45 feet from front to back. There were four rooms and a chimney in every room to keep everyone warm in winter. A 12-foot hall with no doors on it ran down the middle of the house from front to back to give everyone a nice cool breeze in the summer. Lots of houses built during that time had the big open hallway. They called the hallway a dogtrot. That type of house was called a dogtrot house.

The house was built on brick pillars so that air

The Sansom home near Black Creek where Emma grew up.

could circulate under the house. A wooden fence surrounded the house, with a gate in the front.

Emma was little but she brought in little things.

Everyone pitched in and soon life was back to normal.

It was a wonderful place for a little girl to play.

Emma picked wildflowers that dotted the roadside. There was land to explore that seemed to almost have no end, and the adventurous Emma wanted to explore it all.

But there was one place that Emma was warned about.

Black Creek.

Sometimes in the afternoons, after the work was

Emma Sansom: Confederate Heroine

Black Creek today near the site of the Sansom Home still runs deep between steep banks.

done, Micajah would walk with Emma down to the creek. He made sure she noticed how steep the banks were and how the water lay in deep black pools.

"Why is it called Black Creek?" she asked.

"So many trees stand tall over the creek that in the fall the leaves fall off into the water," Micajah explained. "The pools are so deep that the current is slow, so the leaves just sink to the bottom instead of getting washed away.

"Once they sink to the bottom," he went on, "they decay and stain the water black."

Some days they walked upstream, up the mountain slope to a high and rocky place. It was a special kind of place, especially after a hard rain. That is when misty spray rose high into the air from the base of Black Creek Falls (Today it is called Noccalula Falls).

The banks were steep and boulders were everywhere. The water rushed over a rocky ledge and fell 90 feet before smashing into the creek bed below. From there it rushed over the boulders until reaching the base of the mountain. Once in the valley, as it passed the Sansom farm where the water had turned black from decaying leaves, the stream flowed so slowly that it seemed to hardly move at all. Except when it rained a lot.

As years passed, the older children married, moved out and started families of their own. After a while, only Rufus, Jennie and Emma were still at home with their parents.

Emma and Rufus attended school in Gadsden along with other farm families. The school was Slack Academy and it was near Second and Chestnut streets beside the Coosa River. Dr. and Mrs. J.W. Slack started the school in 1852, the same year that the Sansoms came to their new farm.

When farm chores were done each day Emma and Rufus explored the hills and the valleys. They soon knew every path along the mountainside. Emma knew

Emma Sansom: Confederate Heroine

her father's fields well and she and Rufus ran barefoot all up and down Black Creek.

Emma knew where it was safe to cross the creek, and where it wasn't. She watched the cows go carefully down the creek bank and make their way through the water to feed on the other side. The cattle always looked for shallow water, because when it rained, Black Creek could be treacherous.

Often Emma's sunbonnet would fly off her head and hang down her back as she ran across their farmland. The sun would make her auburn hair shine. She was not a large child, but being the youngest of twelve, she was not afraid of anything and was curious about everything.

When she and Rufus weren't running barefoot they were riding their horses along the Tuscaloosa road, which ran close below their house. Stagecoaches bound for Huntsville and Chattanooga passed along the road. The Sansoms loved living in Alabama and Micajah bought more land. In just a few years, the farm grew from its original 40 acres to 280 acres.

It was 1859 and Emma was twelve. Gadsden was still a small village, but growing.

Then something started to change. No one could

really say when things started to change. It was just something that the children noticed after a while.

The people still were friendly and helpful to each other. They still got together to do things. But it wasn't like before. Now, it seemed like every time friends or families got together the grown-ups were always whispering in small groups.

Once Emma heard her father talking to Rufus, telling him that he might have to make an important decision soon. It was something to do with politics. Emma didn't understand what it was all about, but she knew it was serious. She read the newspaper whenever they could get one. There was lots of news about arguments between the northern states and the southern states.

December of 1859 was cold, colder than usual. It was bitter that Christmas Eve, and Emma was glad to get in the house where it was warm after finishing her morning chores.

Suddenly Emma knew something was wrong. The house was too quiet. Her mother came in, tears streaming down her face.

"What's wrong!?" the children asked their mother all at once.

Lamila reached out her arms to gather Emma,

Emma Sansom: Confederate Heroine

Jennie and Rufus so she could hold them close.

She brushed back her tears and told them the news: "Your Pa is dead."

There was no accident or injury. It was just one of those sad things.

Margie Dover Ross

Changes

IT WAS THE SADDEST OF TIMES for the Sansom family.

But the Sansoms were strong.

They knew Micajah would want them to keep the farm going and that is just what they did.

Rufus took on many of the planting chores and Emma helped as much as she could with the animals while Rufus tended to the crops.

The next year, political fights were everywhere. In Congress there were battles between the slave states in the South and free states in the North. Each part of the country was trying to get more political power than the other part of the country.

At the Alabama capitol in Montgomery, some representatives were talking about voting Alabama out of the United States and joining other southern states in a Confederacy. It would mean forming a new gov-

Emma Sansom: Confederate Heroine

ernment, just for the southern states.

Across Alabama, everyone was talking about what would happen if Abraham Lincoln were elected president. Would the southern states really try to get out of the United States? Emma knew what the fussing was about. She was old enough to understand, and she had heard her father talking to Rufus about the North/South troubles before he died.

She knew Abraham Lincoln wanted to abolish slavery if he won the election. Even though her family did not own slaves, she knew that the South depended on slaves to work the large cotton plantations in the southern part of the state.

Most farmers in north Alabama did not own slaves. The farms in the north Alabama valleys were smaller than the giant plantations to the south. The north Alabama farmers could tend to their farms without slave help.

Some of them didn't believe in slavery and were against the South's efforts to get out of the United States.

The Sansoms didn't like the rumors that there might be a war between the North and South if Lincoln was elected president. They were afraid that if war came, Rufus would want to enlist. Lamila, Jennie and Emma hoped that the states could solve their problems without going to war. Maybe they could pass new laws to make everyone happy. Or maybe both sides could give in just a little bit to keep people from getting killed.

On November 6, 1860, Abraham Lincoln was elected president.

In December 1860, South Carolina voted to pull out of the United States. Other southern states started doing the same thing. They called it seceding from the Union.

Alabama seceded January 11, 1861.

In February, representatives from all the southern states that had pulled out met in Montgomery, Alabama and formed the Confederate States of America. On February 18, Jefferson Davis was inaugurated as President of the Confederate States of America. Soon afterward they began raising an army.

The thing that Lamila, Jennie and Emma dreaded most had come. Rufus said he wanted to join the Confederate army. They couldn't talk him out of it. Rufus had made up his mind to enlist in the second company of Gadsden, Nineteenth Alabama Infantry. He was going to fight for Alabama.

Emma, Jennie and their mother told Rufus

Emma Sansom: Confederate Heroine

goodbye, and with dread in their stomachs watched as he rode down the road, and crossed the wooden bridge over Black Creek that he and his sisters had played on as children.

Emma put her hand up to her forehead to shield her eyes from the sun and watched Rufus until he was out of sight.

Nathan Bedford Forrest

NATHAN BEDFORD FORREST was a grown man before Emma Sansom was born.

He did not know her, not even that she existed.

But he was the man who made things happen that changed Emma's life forever.

Nathan Bedford Forrest and his twin sister, Fannie, were born in the backwoods of Tennessee on July 13, 1821, to William and Mariam Beck Forrest. They named him Nathan after his grandfather and Bedford for the county he was born in.

He and Fannie were William and Mariam's oldest children, and other children soon followed. Seven more. But only six of the nine children survived to adulthood. Besides Bedford and Fannie, there were seven sons and two daughters: John, William, Aaron, Jesse, Jeffrey, Milly and Mary.

Emma Sansom: Confederate Heroine

Forrest was six feet one a half inches tall when he was a teenager. Bedford, as he was called, had piercing gray eyes. His mother called them stubborn eyes.

As a boy, Bedford enjoyed hunting with his cousins Wallace and Orrin Beck. They were older than Bedford and both boys were good hunters. Wallace and Orrin taught Bedford to sneak up quietly on animals and shoot when the animals least expected it. Bedford learned quickly how to surprise an animal in the woods.

One day when all three boys were out hunting, they heard dogs barking. Suddenly, a deer darted across the trail in front of them. The dogs ran right behind it, teeth bared and tongues hanging out ready for the kill. No hunter appeared.

"Those are the meanest hounds in Bedford County," exclaimed Bedford.

"They belong to Mr. Patterson," Wallace said, as he nodded his head in agreement.

"He lets those dogs run wild. He never trains his huntin' hounds," Orrin chimed in.

"They chase our horses every time we pass the Patterson place," said Bedford.

Orrin looked up as he saw the dogs run into the woods and shook his head. "Those dogs look like they would kill anything that got in their way."

"I hope it's not me," Bedford said as they started down the trail after the dogs were gone

When Bedford got home that evening he asked his mother if he could ride his uncle's horse, Storm King, to a friend's house the next day.

Uncle Jonathan Forrest knew that Bedford had a special talent for breaking horses, so he had brought Storm King for Bedford to train.

Storm King had only recently become gentle enough to ride. Bedford couldn't wait to show his friend, Andrew McLauren.

Mrs. Forrest thought about it for a minute and then said, "All right, son." She knew once his mind was made up he would have taken the horse anyway. Mariam knew where he got that stubborn determination. She was the same way.

The next morning Bedford was up early, quickly finishing his morning chores so he could ride Storm King to Andy's. Bedford put only a bridle on the horse. He did not need a saddle.

They took off down the road. Both boy and horse enjoyed the fast run. Before he got to the Patterson farm, he slowed Storm King to a walk.

He listened closely for old Patterson's wild hounds. Bedford held his breath. He didn't hear any sound at all. *Maybe they've gone hunting*, he thought to himself. Bedford relaxed and slowly let his breath out. He and Storm King passed the Patterson farm quietly. Bedford held the bridle loosely and combed his fingers through Storm King's mane.

"Arf! Arf! Arf! Arf!" It was the Patterson hounds barking furiously and flying out of the woods straight for Bedford and the colt.

"Giddiup!" Bedford yelled as he reached quickly for the rein. He could feel his knees gripping Storm King's sides as he struggled to stay on the back of the colt. The hounds nipped at the colt's heels.

Bedford could hear his heart pounding in his throat.

Storm King was frightened and reared up on two legs.

With no saddle, Bedford began slipping.

"NOOOOO!" Bedford yelled loudly as he landed on the hard ground with a thud. Storm King took off at a full gallop for home.

Bedford covered his head with his hands and closed his eyes. He knew the dogs would be on him.

Instead, he heard only their whines as they began running the other way with their tails tucked between their legs.

Bedford looked up in surprise and heard laughter

in the distance.

It was Mr. Patterson. He started toward Bedford to help him up out of the dust. He slapped his hand against his britches and laughed some more. "I didn't know who was more scairt—you, the dogs, or the colt. I ain't never seen so many scared animals in all my life. When you hit that ground with a thud, those hounds were so startled they took off every which way. It shore was funny." Mr. Patterson couldn't stop laughing.

Bedford started laughing too. Since he was so scared, he didn't know if he was laughing to keep from crying or laughing because it was so funny.

Either way, from that time on he knew the importance of surprising the enemy.

Bedford's father was a blacksmith and, like the Sansoms, his family also farmed. They moved from Tennessee to Mississippi in 1834 and, again like the Sansoms, they took over Indian lands that had been opened up for settlers. Bedford was 13 years old. The new land was in Tippah County, not far from the Tennessee state line.

Unlike the Sansom family, the Forrests did not prosper on their new Mississippi land. Bedford was 16 when his father died of fever. It was a terrible time.

Emma Sansom: Confederate Heroine

Many people in their village were sick with the fever. All of Bedford's sisters came down with it and died.

Bedford had the fever too. But he got well. Once recovered he found himself head of the household, with six brothers, a fatherless baby and a mother who was now a widow to care for.

The family was poor, and had to work hard to survive. Bedford taught himself to make shoes and buckskin leggings from animal hides for his younger brothers.

As a boy, Bedford had a reputation for being the nosiest child playing and he could holler the loudest when he was getting a whipping by his mother. Miriam Forrest was tough, and was quick to whip her children if they disobeyed. Even when Bedford and his brothers came home and visited as young men they were afraid to disobey her.

On a furlough from the army, one of Bedford's eighteen-year-old brothers had been asked by Mariam to take some corn to the mill for grinding. He refused and told her to get one of the slaves to do it. She went outside, pulled a switch off a bush and went to his room. She yanked him out of bed and switched him good. Once punished, he got on his horse right quick and took the corn to the mill.

In was in the Mississippi settlement that Bedford almost lost his mother.

Mariam and Bedford's Aunt Fannie—who Bedford's twin sister was named after—had gone to visit their nearest neighbors nine miles away.

The neighbors were so excited to have company that they shared some new baby chicks with them. Not everyone had chickens in the frontier settlements. Those who did enjoyed fresh eggs and fried chicken—special treats in those days.

Mariam and Fannie were thrilled to get the baby chicks because they did not have any on their farm.

As they were riding back home, it was beginning to get dark in the Mississippi forest.

The woods at night were a nervous kind of place. Fannie and Mariam should have left for home earlier. But things seemed OK. They were only about a mile from their cabin.

Then the horses began acting strange. They got faster and faster, and the women couldn't hold them back.

"Mariam, what is wrong with the horses?" Fannie asked in a scared voice.

An animal scream pierced the night.

Mariam and Fannie looked at each other in fear.

Emma Sansom: Confederate Heroine

They knew the scream. They peered into the tree branches overhead. They could see nothing, but they knew it was there.

It was a panther, hungry and just waiting for its chance at them.

It must have smelled the chicks. Mariam tightened her grip on the basket of peeping chicks.

"Let go of the chicks, Mariam, the panther is going to jump!" Fannie screamed.

Mariam just strengthened her grip on the basket.

Just then, the panther sprang down from a tree onto the road right in front of the horses.

Fannie turned her horse sharply so he would go around the panther.

She stood up in the stirrups, whipping her horse to a gallop and screamed out, "Bedford! Bedford! A panther is getting your Ma!"

Mariam had been right behind Fannie but her horse reeled and fell over into a creek that ran in front of the cabin.

Mariam, the horse and the panther were scrambling in the water. The panther leaped at Mariam, raking its claws deep into her shoulder, and trying to get to the baby chicks.

Mariam could feel her blood soak through her dress as she pulled the horse back to its feet. She dashed toward the safety of the cabin, still tightly clutching the basket of chicks.

The panther ran away. It probably intended to return later that night for the kill.

Bedford rushed to the door to help his mother. He hollered at his brothers to take care of the horses. Fannie and Bedford helped Mariam over to the bed. Bedford got the turpentine and began tenderly dabbing at his mother's wounds. The turpentine stung terribly, but Mariam didn't cry.

Once he had cleaned his mother's wounds, Bedford took his father's flintlock down from the fireplace.

"Where ya' think you're goin', son?" Ma demanded.

"I'm goin' to kill that beast if he stays on this earth," Bedford answered.

Mariam knew he was going to do just what he said. She could see those stubborn gray eyes narrowed to slits. She knew Bedford had to battle the panther.

Bedford left the cabin with the dogs yelping hot on the panther's trail. As the barking faded, Mariam wondered how Bedford would keep up with the panther. It had been so quick.

Bedford managed to keep up throughout night, but after a while even Bedford began wondering how

Emma Sansom: Confederate Heroine

long he could go on. Suddenly the dogs stopped.

The panther was treed.

Quickly, Bedford ran to the spot and raised the flintlock.

Then he changed his mind and slowly lowered the gun. He decided to wait until daybreak so there would be no chance of missing. Bedford found himself a place in a large tree root. He swatted mosquitoes until dawn.

The dogs circled the bottom of the tree. The panther snarled down at them. The panther thought the dogs were his only enemy. Bedford just waited quietly and out of the panther's sight.

Daybreak came. Bedford aimed the flintlock right at the panther's heart. It took only one bullet and the panther fell from the tree, without ever knowing that its real enemy wasn't the dogs at all.

Bedford skinned the panther, and took the skin to his mother.

He did not know it then, but that would not be the last time he would use those frontier skills.

He would need them again, and in a much bigger battle.

And he would find Emma Sansom right in the middle of it.

The War

NATHAN BEDFORD FORREST NEVER WAS a model citizen.

He was good at school, but he didn't like it, except for arithmetic, just a little bit.

He always wanted to be out fishing or hunting, instead of in school.

He was terrible at spelling and writing, and was forever getting into fights.

He quit school to help his mother with the farm.

Bedford grew to be a restless young man, anxious to leave the farm and learn a trade. His mother saw that it was time for Bedford to go, and she told him that he should leave to find his way in the world. His brothers were nearly grown and could help her take care of the farm.

Uncle Jonathan asked him to come to Hernando, Mississippi, and learn the livestock trade. Bedford

Emma Sansom: Confederate Heroine

agreed and quickly became an excellent horse and cattle trader.

Bedford also discovered something else. He found that he liked to dress up now and then, comb his coal-black hair and beard and visit friends on Sunday afternoons. All of a sudden, Bedford began liking things neat and orderly.

It was there in Hernando, while out visiting one Sunday afternoon that Bedford happened upon a carriage stuck in a huge mud hole.

Two women sat in the carriage while the driver whipped the horses. He wanted the horses to work harder to pull the carriage out of the mud, but no matter how hard he whipped and how hard they tried, the carriage would not budge.

Bedford could not stand the sight and he leaped from his horse shouting, "Stop lashing those poor horses. That is no way to get out of this mud hole."

Then he waded into the mud, took off his hat and introduced himself.

"Ladies, my name is Bedford Forrest and if you allow me to carry you to dry ground, I will get your carriage out of the mud hole."

"Thank you. My name is Mrs. Montgomery and this is my daughter, Miss Mary Ann Montgomery," the older lady answered. He carried the mother and her daughter to a dry spot, then waded back into the mud.

"Get back up in that carriage and lead those animals without lashing them," he ordered the driver.

He then put his shoulder to the carriage and gave a big shove. The wheels soon worked free and the animals were able to get the carriage on dry ground.

Bedford was covered with mud, but before riding off for new clothes he could not help but notice how pretty Miss Mary Ann Montgomery was.

Nor could he resist, even covered with mud, asking Mrs. Montgomery if he could call on Miss Mary Ann the next day.

Mrs. Montgomery told Bedford that he could. She didn't say so right then, but she already thought Bedford was wonderful for getting their carriage out of the mud.

Forrest soon became a regular visitor at the Montgomery house. He wanted to marry Mary Ann and decided to ask for her hand in marriage. Her uncle, Samuel Montgomery Cowan, was Mary Ann's guardian. He also was pastor of the Cumberland Presbyterian Church. He knew Bedford had a reputation for rowdy living.

"Why, I couldn't possibly consent." Cowan said when Bedford asked permission to marry Mary Ann. "You cuss and gamble and Mary Ann is a Christian

Emma Sansom: Confederate Heroine

girl."

"I know," answered Bedford with a big smile, "that's why I want to marry her!"

Cowan gave in and one month later, on September 25, 1845, Mary Ann Montgomery became Mrs. Nathan Bedford Forrest. She was nineteen years old.

They had two children, a boy named William Montgomery and a girl named Frances, who they called Fanny. At first, they lived in Hernando, but in 1851 they moved to Memphis, Tennessee, where Bedford tried all sorts of jobs.

He ran a store and a stage coach line. He sold cattle and horses. And slaves.

He got rich buying and selling slaves to the many cotton plantation owners of the Mississippi River delta.

Bedford decided to quit buying and selling slaves, and to take those he owned at the time and set up a plantation. He bought land in Coahoma County, Mississippi, and began growing cotton. He did well with cotton, raising a thousand bales and earning $30,000 in 1861.

It was the last crop he would oversee for several years.

South Carolina had pulled out of the Union, and Bedford knew that a terrible struggle lay ahead. Even worse to him, if the South lost that struggle he could lose everything he had.

One by one the other Southern states followed South Carolina in seceding from the United States.

Bedford knew he had to join the fight.

He enlisted as a private in White's Tennessee Mounted Rifles along with his brother, Jeffrey, and his fifteen-year-old son, William.

Shortly after he signed up, some important citizens from Memphis went to the state capital at Nashville to convince the governor that Nathan Bedford Forrest should not be allowed to enlist as a private.

They told the governor that Bedford was a good fighter and a leader, and that he should be made an officer.

The governor listened and Bedford was promoted to Lieutenant Colonel. He also was told that he could begin recruiting a battalion of mounted rangers.

Bedford placed an advertisement for volunteers in the *Avalanche*, a Memphis newspaper. He then bought 500 pistols, 100 saddles and other equipment.

Men from throughout the area enlisted with Bedford, even though most of them knew he had no real military training.

What they knew was that Bedford was a fighter

Emma Sansom: Confederate Heroine

and that he had been raised on the harsh frontier. Many of the volunteers were from the frontier too. They didn't know much about the army either, but they knew horses and surviving in the woods and how to fight to win. They knew a man like Bedford wouldn't let them down.

Battles came quickly.

Bedford and his men soon built a reputation for fearlessness. He didn't fight like a trained military man. Instead, he fought like a frontiersman with surprise attacks and tricks to catch the Yankees when they least expected it.

Bedford even quarreled with other Confederate officers, and made them mad. And he was rough with any soldier who was afraid to fight. But Bedford did not care. His men fought hard, and he treated them well.

More than once the war almost got the best of Bedford.

In the winter of 1862 he was helping defend Fort Donelson on the Cumberland River in middle Tennessee.

The weather was terrible, and the Union soldiers had the fort surrounded.

Many officers told Bedford he should surrender.

He refused, and told his men that they could surrender if they wanted or try to sneak out of the fort with him. Not one of his men surrendered. They all escaped from the fort down an unguarded road.

Nathan Bedford Forrest, "the Wizard of the Saddle."

In April of the same year he and his cavalry were fighting in Tennessee at the Battle of Shiloh. Bedford and his horse were both shot. A bullet had hit Bedford in the side, just above his hipbone Later that night the horse died. Forrest survived.

He was a great cavalry leader. The Confederates called him "the Wizard of the Saddle." The Yankees called him "That Devil Forrest."

He was sneaky and tough and he never gave up, just like when he stalked that panther years before.

Emma Sansom soon would find out in a very personal way just how Nathan Bedford Forrest earned his nicknames.

Yankees

GENERAL WILLIAM ROSECRANS was a fine soldier.

He had attended West Point, and taught there before leaving the Army to become an engineer.

When the Civil War began he went back into the Army to fight for the United States, and in the spring of 1863 he found himself in charge of the Army of the Cumberland.

This was a huge army of Union soldiers headquartered in Tennessee. Their job was to fight the Confederate soldiers in Tennessee, plus parts of Mississippi, Alabama and Georgia.

On the Confederate side was Major General Braxton Bragg. He was in charge of the Confederate Army of Tennessee.

Soldiers who were assigned to the armies of the two generals often fought each other. Rosecrans had won several battles in the middle part of Tennessee, but Bragg still was in charge in Chattanooga. A railroad from Atlanta, Georgia, to Chattanooga kept Bragg equipped with medicine, food and ammunition. As long as the rail line operated, Rosecrans was going to have a lot of trouble whipping him.

One of General Rosecrans' cleverest officers, Colonel Abel D. Streight, had an idea of how Rosecrans could defeat Bragg: He would loop around behind Chattanooga, through Alabama, into Georgia and tear up the railroad so there would be no way to send supplies from Atlanta to Chattanooga.

Without supplies and ammunition, Bragg would be easier to whip.

It was a risky idea. But General Rosecrans liked it anyway. He sent a message to Colonel Streight to start making plans for the raid.

This is what Streight told the general: He would

Abel Streight, the Union colonel who led the raid across Alabama.

Emma Sansom: Confederate Heroine

take 2,000 Union soldiers on horseback by boat down the Cumberland River from middle Tennessee, and then walk a short distance to the Tennessee River. From there, boats would take them just past Tuscumbia, in the northwest corner of Alabama. That is where they would unload, and then ride their horses all the way back across north Alabama to Rome, a town in northeast Georgia. Two streams come together to form the Coosa River in Rome. The railroad from Atlanta to Chattanooga ran right through Rome, and had to cross the river there. When he got to Rome, Streight would tear up the river bridge and the trains would no longer be able to take supplies to General Bragg in Chattanooga.

On the way to Rome, Streight added, his soldiers would destroy any factories making guns, ammunition or other supplies that the Confederates needed. And they would burn all the bridges behind them as they rode toward Rome.

The risky part was that Colonel Streight and his Union soldiers would have to travel fast for a long way through enemy country without getting caught. Still, he thought it had a good chance of working.

Colonel Streight was no professional soldier. Before the war he had been in the publishing business in Indiana. But he had studied the Alabama area, and he had some special soldiers.

They were men from north Alabama who did not believe in the Confederacy. When the war started, they went north and joined the Union army. These Alabama Yankees knew north Alabama well because they had grown up there. They would be able to guide Streight's troops through the winding mountain trails, and keep them at the edge of the forests where they would be hard to notice. With the help of his Alabama Yankees, Streight thought the plan would work.

How could he ever have known that his raid would take him right past the Sansom farm on Black Creek.

Or that the entire fate of his raid would rest in the hands of a little auburn-haired 15-year-old girl.

Emma Sansom.

General Rosecrans told Streight to get his men and supplies together.

Streight was pleased that the general was going to let him lead the raid. He was an adventurous man and willing to take great risks for a cause he believed in passionately. He was going after some rebel boys on their own homeland and he would destroy their railroad and cut off their supply line.

Emma Sansom: Confederate Heroine

He was only 34 years old, strong and broad-chested. He wore a beard and was considered tough by his men. When the war broke out he took on responsibility for recruiting the 51st Regiment of Indiana Infantry.

Even though he was an infantryman or a foot soldier as they were sometimes referred to, he admired the Confederate Calvary raids of Nathan Bedford Forrest. And he knew that he would have to put his foot soldiers on horses if they were to move across Alabama fast enough to reach the railroad at Rome before getting caught by the enemy rebel army.

Instead of horses, he got mules.

It seemed like a good idea at the time. Mules can live on less food than horses, and are tougher.

But these mules were not tougher. Many of them were very young and poorly trained; some even wild and not ready to ride. Others were sick with distemper and dying. A dozen died before they could even be loaded on the boats at Nashville.

Things were starting off badly.

Streight kept what mules he could, but there were not enough for all of his soldiers. By the time they reached Eastport, Mississippi, just west of Tuscumbia, more mules had died.

At Eastport, Streight planned a trick that he thought he could use to slip into the hills of north Alabama without the Confederates noticing anything.

It was another plan that backfired.

Streight's trick was to join up with a Union army that already was at Eastport. Streight's men, plus the bigger army which was being led by General Grenville M. Dodge would pretend to start an invasion into Alabama.

Streight knew that the 4th Alabama Infantry was nearby. He also knew that when he and General Dodge started moving into Alabama, the 4th Alabama and its commander, General P.D. Roddy, would fight back. When that happened, Streight's plan was to break away from General Dodge's army and slip off and ride toward Rome.

The mules messed up his plan.

After they got off the boats the mules hee-hawed constantly. And they seemed to be even louder at night.

General Roddy had sent some 4th Alabama Infantry scouts to Eastport to see what the Yankees were doing.

They could hear the mules, and sneaked up close to see what all the noise was about.

They got so close they could hear the Yankee

Emma Sansom: Confederate Heroine

soldiers trying to get the mules to be quiet.

The harder they tried to quiet the mules the louder the mules hee-hawed.

The Confederate soldiers hid in the bushes nearby and tried hard not to laugh out loud.

Then they got an idea that they thought would really be fun. They sneaked right up into the middle of all the mules, then jumped up and began yelling.

One thousand three hundred wild-eyed mules panicked.

They ran in every direction. The Confederate scouts grabbed some of the mules and rode into the hills with them before the Union soldiers could figure out what was going on.

It took all night for the Union soldiers to round up the mules that the Confederate scouts had not stolen.

They got most of them back.

But they lost their chance to surprise anyone.

Thanks to the mules, the Confederates knew something was about to happen.

Rebels

EVEN AS STREIGHT'S MEN SEARCHED the hills and hollows for their scattered mules, General Bragg was ordering one of his finest cavalry officers to go to Decatur to help General Roddy and the 4th Alabama.

Something was going on in northwest Alabama. He wasn't sure what. But he wanted Nathan Bedford Forrest there to help take care of things.

April 23, 1863. Forrest's cavalry mounted and rode to Roddy's aid.

April 24, 1863. Streight and his men took the mules they could round up and met General Dodge's army in Tuscumbia.

There, Dodge gave them 200 more mules and six wagons to haul their food and ammunition.

Then another bad thing happened to Streight. Almost a fourth of his men had gotten too sick to go on. General Dodge let them stay with his army to get well. It left Streight with 1,500 men for his raid across

Emma Sansom: Confederate Heroine

Alabama.

The fake Union invasion of northwest Alabama began.

On April 26, Forrest crossed the Tennessee River at Brown's Ferry near Courtland, Alabama, and joined Roddy's cavalry just in time for a fight with General Dodge

The much larger Yankee army easily pushed the Confederate soldiers across Town Creek and it looked as though Streight's tricky plan to slip away from the battle unnoticed was going to work.

But it didn't.

General Roddy knew how important it was to always have scouts keeping an eye on things. One of those scouts saw Streight and his 1,500 men break away from General Dodge's army, cross Town Creek and head south, away from the battle.

The scout found General Forrest and told him what he had seen.

Forrest knew instantly something was up, and he intended to find out what it was.

He quickly got ready to chase after Streight. He chose his best horses and harnesses, and doubled the teams that were to pull the cannons along. He had three days of food prepared for his troops, and then, as the rains poured down on them, he gave his men more ammunition and a stern warning: "No matter what else gets wet, you must keep your cartridge-box dry."

The spring rains fell in torrents. Streight's army slipped away from Dodge's army just before midnight on April 26. "We marched in heavy rains and mud on to Russellville...and towards Moulton," he said later. "The road conditions were terrible. Many of my men were on foot, not having any mules or horses available for them. Some of these men carried saddles, in case we were able to acquire animals...by buying from local farmers who were Union sympathizers or animals captured in small battles in the rear guard with the enemy."

"When I left General Dodge, (the town of) Moulton was about 40 miles away and I felt like we would be able to make it by the next night. The rains were too heavy and the roads were too hard to manage."

Streight did not make Moulton by the next night. He had to stop so that his soldiers who were having to walk could catch up. They camped at a place called Mount Hope, about 15 miles east of Moulton, and waited.

Emma Sansom: Confederate Heroine

Across the state in east Alabama the rains muddied the road that passed in front of the Sansom farm. The waters roared over Black Creek Falls, down the steep slopes of Lookout Mountain and into Black Creek.

The usually still deep pools in the creek quickly became deeper and swift. The steep clay banks turned to slippery glass. The waters rose so high over the soft mud bottom that only one spot remained where the cows could ford the creek to feed on the other side.

But it was just another gray, rainy day. There was no fighting going on around the Sansom home. Tuscumbia and New Hope were a long way away.

By 10 the next morning, Streight's foot soldiers had caught up. They moved on toward Moulton, and got there just at dark. About midnight, when most people were asleep and his army would be protected by the darkness, Streight headed out again—eastward for Blountsville.

The roads still were deep mud, but the rains stopped. When it did, the soldiers were a lot happier and didn't seem to mind the mud so much.

By April 29 Streight had reached a place called Day's Gap at the base of Sand Mountain. It seemed

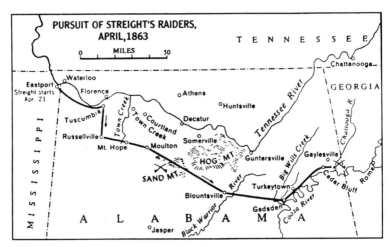

The route of the raid across Alabama.

that he and his men had made a clean getaway. There were no signs that any Confederate troops were following him. The soldiers were excited that the raid was going to work.

Along the way from Moulton they took horses and mules from farmers, and destroyed some wagons loaded with food.

Streight was so filled with confidence he decided to give his men a good night's sleep at Day's Gap, so they would be well rested for the trek over Sand Mountain.

As Streight's men slept, Forrest's men were riding. They came through Moulton less than a day after Streight's men had left.

Emma Sansom: Confederate Heroine

Catching the Enemy

IT WAS JUST AFTER MIDNIGHT on Thursday morning, April 30, and Forrest was only four miles from the mouth of Day's Gap. He knew better than to ride into the gap without sending scouts to see what lay ahead.

Forrest called for his brother, Captain William Forrest, and General Roddy. "Keep right on down the road," he told them, "and get up close to the enemy and see what they are doing." He told the rest of his men to get a good night's sleep.

It did not take long for William Forrest and Roddy to find the Yankee camp. They soon came within sight of their campfires and immediately rode back to tell Forrest that they had found the enemy at the foot of the gorge. Forrest did not attack just then. He wanted his men rested and alert. He intended to take on

Streight the next morning.

Had he waited until morning, Forrest would not have had to send his brother and Roddy to scout the Yankee camp. Once the sun came up every soldier in Forrest's cavalry knew where the camp was.

Streight's mules were hee-hawing so loud that everyone for miles around knew where the Yankees were camped. The Confederate soldiers could not help but laugh.

At dawn that Thursday, Streight's men broke camp and started the long and winding climb up Sand Mountain. The column of wagons and mules and soldiers looked like a giant snake twisting its way up the rocky trail toward the top of the mountain.

Boom!

Streight spun around toward the explosion.

Boom! Boom!

It was Forrest. On the attack. Firing his cannons into Streight's rear guard.

They were anxious for the fight. Too anxious as it turned out.

Forrest's brother, William, General Roddy and several scouts dashed out ahead of Forrest's main army, chasing Union soldiers up the mountain. They rode too far too fast. Streight had quickly set up an

Emma Sansom: Confederate Heroine

ambush, and William Forrest, General Roddy and their scouts rode right into it.

The fighting was fierce. William Forest was shot in the leg. Several of the Confederate cannons were captured.

Forrest clinched his jaw and retreated.

He was furious.

Not only had Forrest lost his first fight with Streight, he also had lost the help of his brother, some of his cannons and ammunition.

He was going to get revenge.

He was going to attack until he had won.

"Whenever you see anything blue, shoot at it," he told his men, "and do all you can to keep up the scare."

Across the mountains they fought the whole day and into the night. Forrest never let up. "The pine trees were very tall, and the darkness of their shade was intense," one of Forrest's men told friends later. "The mountain where the enemy was posted was steep, and as we charged again and again under Forrest's own lead—it was a grand spectacle.

"It seemed that the fires which blazed from (the Union soldiers') muskets were almost long enough to reach our faces," he said. "There was one advantage in being below them: they often fired above our heads in the darkness."

It was near 10 p.m. when Forrest finally pushed back the Union soldiers and got his cannons back. But they were of no use. The Union soldiers had torn them up so the Confederates could not use them again.

The shooting died down as Streight pulled back to a place where the woods and undergrowth were very thick. This thicket, he decided, was a great place to ambush the Confederates.

This time Forrest was more cautious.

He sent out a few men to find where the Union soldiers were hiding. But they didn't find the Yankees. One of their horses did. The scouts were about to ride right into the ambush when the horse began sniffing the air and acting up.

It smelled Yankees. The scout figured out quickly why the horse was acting so strangely and rode back to tell Forrest where the Union soldiers were hiding.

It was dark, near midnight. Forrest quietly moved some of his cannons near the thicket and aimed them right at it. The Yankees didn't even know they were there. Not until Forrest gave the order to fire.

Belching fire and smoke, and with a deafening roar, the cannon fire pierced the night. Union soldiers scattered in every direction. The two armies traded gunfire until nearly 1 a.m., before Streight decided to

Emma Sansom: Confederate Heroine

pull back again and make a run for the town of Blountsville.

He thought that if he could break away from Forrest, that the Rebels might hold up in the mountains for a day or two to rest, get new supplies and take care of their wounded.

Once he got to Blountsville, Streight thought that he could get supplies and maybe even some horses.

It was Friday morning, May Day. It was a festival day in Blountsville; a time for the people to relax, to play, to have a big community picnic and to get their mind off the war for a few hours.

From all around the area families were coming to town on their best horses and mules with picnic baskets filled with all kinds of food and desserts.

General Streight spoiled the picnic.

The Union soldiers took the horses and the picnic food. They found other supplies in the town's stores and took it.

They loaded some supplies on wagons and set them on fire so Forrest's men couldn't use them.

Then they ate the picnic food and rested a while. All the citizens of Blountsville could do was look on in anger.

Streight didn't know how determined a man

Forrest could be when he got mad. The Confederates had rested only a little while, and almost caught Streight right there in Blountsville. They got there so quickly, in fact, they were able to save some supplies from the wagons that Streight's men had set afire.

Streight was on the run.

Next in his path was rain-swollen Black Creek. And only one place to cross: a wooden bridge.

If only he could make Black Creek before Forrest closed in, he could burn the bridge and hold Forrest back. It just might buy him enough time to get to Rome and destroy the railroad bridge.

Emma Sansom: Confederate Heroine

To Black Creek

FORREST KNEW THE YANKEES had the advantage. The Union soldiers were across the Warrior River and moving fast.

Forrest decided not to cross the river with his whole army right away. Instead, he picked just 100 of his best men to cross the river and shoot at the Yankees all night long so they could not rest.

Then Forrest told the remainder of his army to get some sleep.

The next morning, Saturday, May 2, Forrest's army crossed the Warrior River and caught up with the hand-picked soldiers who had been shooting at the Union soldiers all night.

The plan was perfect. Streight had traveled all night without sleeping because they could never get away from the little skirmishes with Forrest's 100 hand-picked men. That special little group had moved along parallel with Streight's column, making Streight believe that it was Forrest's whole army. He feared that Forrest was trying to get around him and block his path to Rome.

Streight was never sure how many men Forrest had. And he could not figure out why they seemed to never get tired.

Streight decided that if his men could keep on moving and stay ahead of the Confederates for just a little longer, they would be able to rest once they crossed the Black Creek bridge and burned it.

At that very moment, Emma and Jennie Sansom were up for Saturday morning chores. There were animals to feed, water to draw from the well, and old Bessie to milk.

Forrest knew it would be a close call whether he could stop Streight before Streight made it to Rome to destroy the bridge.

He didn't want to take a chance that the people of Rome would be unprepared if he wasn't able to stop the Union soldiers. He called for a rider and wrote a note to be taken to Rome. The spelling was not perfect, but the message was clear:

to the authorities at Rome, Georgia...theirs is a Federal Force of fifteen Hundred calvary Marching on

Emma Sansom: Confederate Heroine

your place and I am pressing them Prepare your selves to Repuls them-they have 2 Mountain Howitsers I will be clost on them I have kild 300 of their men they air running for their lives!.!

The race across Alabama was at full speed. Streight's men were on a mad dash for Black Creek. Only one thing stood between them and the Black Creek bridge.

The Sansom farm.

Margie Dover Ross

Emma Sansom: Confederate heroine

Face to Face

EMMA SANSOM STRAINED ON TIPTOE to watch the blue coated Yankees thunder down the road toward her house.

"Run to the house," she told Jennie in a hushed voice. "Tell Mother to stay inside. Maybe they just want water for their horses and mules." Jennie ran inside quickly to tell her mother and then came back outside to see about Emma.

"The Yankee company formed a long blue line as they whooshed past sister and I and went galloping toward the bridge," she told friends later. "Pretty soon a great crowd of them came along."

A cloud of dust boiled up and surrounded Emma like a great fog, then after a while they all had galloped by and the dust began to settle.

When it cleared enough, all Emma could see was blue. Blue uniforms on every side of her.

She did not move. She clutched her milk bucket tightly.

Her heart pounded as she looked up.

Right into the eyes of a Yankee.

"We need some water," he said. "Would you bring us some water?"

It was the enemy, but they were three—two teenage girls and their mother—facing a battle-hardened army of Yankee soldiers

"Sister and I each took a bucket of water and gave it to them at the gate," Emma told friends later. "My hands were trembling as I handed over the water bucket, but I steadied it so they would not see my fear."

"Where's your father?" said one of the Yankee men gruffly.

"He's dead," Emma answered.

"Do you have any brothers?" he asked.

"Six," she said, but did not tell more.

"Where are they?" the Yankee wanted to know.

Emma was tired of the Yankees. Her hands were not shaking any more. She wasn't afraid any more. She didn't like the Yankees on her farm. She didn't like their questions. And she wasn't going to put up with it any longer.

"They are in the Confederate Army," she said, with new courage in her voice.

"Do they think the South will whip?" the Yankee asked in a tone that let her know that he did not believe that the South could win.

"They do," she answered without hesitating for even a moment.

There was fire in her blue-gray eyes, and she stared with disdain squarely at his face.

"What do you think about it?" the Yankee asked in an arrogant tone. He was just making fun of this teenager. He was trying to make her mad. And he was succeeding.

"I think God is on our side and we will win,"

Emma Sansom: Confederate Heroine

Emma answered.

"You do?" he said, as his lip curled up in a sneer. "Well, if you had seen us whip Colonel Roddy the other day and run him across the Tennessee River, you would have thought God was on the side of the best artillery."

The Union soldiers started getting off their mules, walked right past Emma and into her house just like it belonged to them. Jennie and Emma walked right in behind them. The Union soldiers searched each room, rummaging through Emma and Jennie's belongings.

They were "looking for firearms and men's saddles. They didn't find anything but a side-saddle and one of them cut the skirts off that," Emma said later.

Just then one of the Union soldiers who had stayed out by the road came in and shouted to those in the house, "You men bring a chunk of fire with you, and get out of that house."

In the kitchen was an iron stove. Mrs. Sansom had built a fire in the stove to heat the top of it where food was cooked in skillets and pans. The men ran quickly and got a small burning hickory log out of the stove. They rushed out with the blazing log, and carried it down the road toward Black Creek. A Union officer told one of the soldiers to stay at the house, while all the others headed toward the creek. The officer looked at Emma, her sister and mother and said, "This guard is for your protection."

As the officer rode away, the three women ran outside and stood on the front porch and peered toward the creek to see what the soldiers were going to do with the fire that they had taken from the stove.

But they could not see all the way to the bridge. A little hill rose up between the house and the bridge, blocking their view of what was going on at the creek.

Even though they could not see, it took only a few moments and they knew the smell that was rising into the air.

Burning wood.

A thin spiral of smoke rose above the trees, right over Black Creek bridge. The Yankees were burning the bridge!

The Sansoms had built a rail fence that ran along their property all the way to the bridge. If the bridge burned, it would catch the rails on fire and burn the fence.

"Come with me," Mrs. Sansom told Jennie and Emma. "We will pull the rails away, so they will not be destroyed."

All three dashed towards the bridge to save the

Emma Sansom: Confederate Heroine

fence railings.

At the top of the hill they stopped running.

Below them, already piled on the bridge and in flames were their fence rails. The Yankees had taken down the rails and piled them on the bridge as firewood. In minutes flames leaped high into the sky.

The Sansom women could see something else down below.

Yankees. They were not riding away.

They were taking cover on the other side of the creek and getting their guns ready to ambush anyone who came along and tried to cross.

Emma, Jennie and Mother turned and slowly started back to the house.

They had taken but a few steps when the looked up to see another Union soldier racing as fast as he could right at them.

Right behind him, galloping hard, dust flying, were more men on horses.

This time, they were men in gray.

Confederate soldiers!

A tall, handsome soldier galloped ahead of the others, his gray cape flowing behind him. "Halt and surrender!" he shouted to the fleeing Yankee. The Union soldier stopped in his tracks, threw up his hands and handed over his gun.

The three women stood dumbfounded in the middle of the road. In a matter of minutes, more than a thousand Union soldiers had dashed past their farm, raided their house, taken fire out of their stove and used their fence rails to build a fire that burned the bridge over their creek. Almost before they could turn around, hundreds more soldiers—this time Confederates—come galloping right behind and capturee a prisoner of war right before their eyes!

The Civil War had come to the Sansom farm.

What would happen next?

The tall officer who had just taken the Union soldier prisoner turned to the three women still standing in the road. "Ladies, do not be alarmed," he said, doing his best to calm them down. "I am General Forrest. I and my men will protect you from harm."

Emma could feel the relief wash over her. "We now knew we were among our own men," she said later. She was confident that Forrest and his men would take care of them.

"Where are the Yankees?" General Forrest asked.

"They have set the bridge on fire and they are standing in line on the other side," Mrs. Sansom answered, "and if you go down that hill they will kill the

Emma Sansom: Confederate Heroine

last one of you."

By this time hundreds of Confederate soldiers were around the girls, their mother and the general. Many of them went on down to the creek. The shooting started at once.

Emma, Jennie and Mrs. Sansom ran for home, with Emma running ahead of the other two.

From the hilltop General Forrest stared at the spiral of smoke curling into the air and knew immediately that he had gotten there only a moment too late. The Yankees had beaten him to Black Creek. He did not have to see the water to know that it was running high and fast. With as much rain as had fallen in the past days it could be no other way.

And now he was stuck fighting Streight's rear guard while his main army dashed for Rome to tear up the railroad.

Was this where it all ended? In this broad green valley at the base of Lookout Mountain, sixty miles from Rome? At the foot of a burning bridge? On the slippery clay bank of a creek too deep to ford?

How could he have come so far, fought so hard and gotten so close, and still lose?

Forrest stared for a long minute toward the bridge, as the sounds of battle rose up louder and louder from the creek. The cursed creek.

He had chased after Streight two-thirds of the way across Alabama and when he finally caught him, that ugly little black stream was holding him back.

If he could not get across quickly, Streight would have time to get to Rome, destroy the railroad and doom General Bragg in Chattanooga.

What could he do?!

Suddenly he wheeled his horse around and galloped back to the Sansom house.

This was not going to be the end.

Nathan Bedford Forrest had no intention of it.

He was going to find a way to win this fight.

He was going to whip Streight's army.

He was going to save that railroad.

He was going to find a way.

He went to the only place that he could think of for help.

Forrest dashed up to the Sansom gate, and there stood young Emma. "Can you tell me where I can get across that creek?" he wanted to know.

"There is an unsafe bridge two miles further down the stream, but I know of a trail about two hundred yards above the bridge on our farm," she said without hesitation, "where our cows used to cross in low

Emma Sansom: Confederate Heroine

water.

"I believe you could get your men over there," she went on, "and if you will have my saddle put on a horse I will show you the way."

Did Forrest trust a 15-year-old girl for such important information? It did not matter. Streight's men were moving toward Rome, and Forrest had no other choice.

"There is no time to saddle a horse; get up here behind me," he told Emma. Across from Emma's house, a dirt bank stood several feet higher than the road. Emma scampered onto the bank. Forrest rode his horse close to the bank and Emma jumped off the bank and onto the general's horse.

She sat tight behind the general, still in the soft blue polka dot cotton dress that she had put on to do her morning chores, and with a blue sun bonnet on her head. The two started off up the hill together.

Mrs. Sansom had not heard all that Emma told the general about the ford, or her daughter's offer to show the general where the ford was.

But she saw the two riding back toward the sound of the shooting and her heart leaped into her throat.

Where was he going with her baby daughter!? Who did he think he was? And what in the world could Emma be thinking riding off with him like that?

Mrs. Sansom came running up the hill. Out of breath, she stopped the two and gasped, "Emma, what do you mean?"

Forrest never gave Emma a chance to answer. "She is going to show me a ford where I can get my men over in time to catch those Yankees before they get to Rome," Forrest told Mrs. Sansom. "Don't be afraid—I will bring her back safe."

With that, two galloped away; Forrest urging the horse on faster and faster. Emma clinging to the general's waist. Mrs. Sansom stood there watching them ride into the conflict, then walked back to the yard. There she and Jennie stood holding tightly to each other, filled with the fear of not knowing what would happen next.

They stood motionless, peering toward the creek until they could no longer see Emma's auburn hair flying in the wind.

The Ford

A SMALL STREAM HAD CUT A GULLY through one of the fields that lay between the Sansom house and the creek.

The field sloped downward toward Black Creek, and the stream spilled into the creek.

The little stream was nothing more than a branch, but along its bank the weeds and bushes grew extra thick because they could get plenty of water there. No one, not even Yankees with guns, could see anyone hiding there.

Emma showed Forrest the field, and he galloped hard toward the thick undergrowth along the branch.

Forrest and Emma rode together right down the branch out of sight.

Forrest slowed the horse to a quiet walk and they moved carefully toward Black Creek, upstream from the burning bridge. Emma leaned around Forrest, watching straight ahead and pointing the way to go.

The gunfire grew louder as they neared Black Creek. Confederates on one side, Union soldiers on the other, shooting across the creek at each other.

From the sound of gunfire and the rush of high water, Forrest knew that they were close. Bullets were beginning to hit around them.

"General Forrest, I think we had better get off the horse, as we are now where we may be seen," Emma told the general. They both slid off the horse and crept through the bushes. The branch flowed into Black Creek just upstream from the ford.

They moved quietly and carefully along the bank until they were right at the ford. Emma was in front, leading the general.

Forrest suddenly stepped between Emma and Union soldiers who they could see on the opposite creek bank. "I am glad to have you for a pilot," he told her, "but I am not going to make breastworks of you." (Breastworks are mounds of dirt that soldiers would get behind to protect themselves from enemy gunfire.)

Cannons and rifle fire exploded all around them. Emma and Forrest had stopped at a steep and slippery spot along the creek. Briars tore at Emmas's hands as she grabbed hold of bushes to keep from sliding away. She had to get the general to the spot where she could show him exactly where his men could ford the creek.

Emma Sansom: Confederate Heroine

The ford was hidden by a thick growth of trees, bushes and vines, but Emma knew how to show General Forrest the exact spot. On the opposite bank was a black gum tree with a special mark on it. Right by that tree was where the cows came out of the ford. Emma pointed out the tree to Geneal Forrest.

"I crouched down and showed him the low water where our cows crossed when the creek was high from heavy rains," Emma told her friends after it was all over. "My hands were shaking as I pointed out to him where to go into the water and where to come out on the other side of the creek bank."

Forrest looked over the spot carefully, but quickly.

"The cannonballs were screaming over so loud that some of his men told us to leave the area immediately and hide in some place out of danger, which we did," Emma said later.

The two worked their way back up the branch, but not far enough.

"General Forrest mounted his horse, pulled me up behind him and began riding fast," Emma said. "Bullets were whizzing past us and one pierced my skirt."

Suddenly a feeling came over Emma. It was that same feeling she had earlier when the Yankee soldier kept asking about her family. In that moment, with bullets flying all around, Emma's fear disappeared.

"I was no longer afraid, even though my heart was pounding and the noise from the cannonballs was deafening," she said. "I could see the Yankees on the other side of Black Creek. The smoke from the bridge curled up in a spiral towards the sky like a snake ready to strike. I took off my sunbonnet and waved it in defiance at the Yankees."

All of a sudden the Yankees stopped shooting. What is that? A girl? A little red-headed girl? That little red-headed girl from the farm just up the road?

"For a moment the Yankees were astonished that I was a girl," said Emma. "They quit shooting and began cheering me for my courage as they watched me ride away."

The quiet lasted a minute. Just enough time for Emma and the general to gallop out of the line of fire. Just as quickly the shooting began again.

Forrest did not take Emma all the way home. He had to get his men across the creek.

The general rode up to a group of his men and called for a sergeant named Alfred Williams, and told the sergeant to make sure that Emma got safely back home to her mother, just as he had promised.

Then the general stopped, just for a moment before riding back to the battle. "What is your name?"

he asked.

"Emma Sansom," she said.

"Would you allow me to cut a lock of your hair," he asked, "so that I might have some small thing to remember you by?"

Emma let the general cut a lock of her hair, and he put it safely away.

Sergeant Williams helped Emma down from the general's horse. He kept her safely back from the gunfire until the shooting stopped. Then he put her up onto his horse to take her home.

The ride back to the farmhouse was slower, and much more careful.

As Emma and Sergeant Williams reached the farm, there was Forrest. "I wrote a note for you," he said, "and left it on your bureau."

Forrest looked sad, and he was. He paused a minute longer and told Emma about something terrible that had just happened.

"One of my bravest men has been killed, and he is laid out in the house. His name is Robert Turner," the general told her. "I want you to see that he buried in some graveyard near here."

Then it was over.

The general mounted his horse, and he and his men rode away and left them all alone.

Margie Dover Ross

Robert Turner's body was laid out on the kitchen table. Jennie and Mother washed the bloodstains out of his uniform so he could be buried in it the next day.

Emma went to her room and found the general's note on the bureau where he left it for her. She picked up the note, slowly unfolded it, and looked at what the general had written:

Hed Quartes in Saddle

May 2. 1863

My highest Regards to Miss Ema Sansom for her Gallant conduct while my forse was Skirmishing with the Federals across "Black Creek" near Gadisden, Alabama

                      N.B. Forrest

                      Brig.Gen.

                      Com'd"gN. Ala.

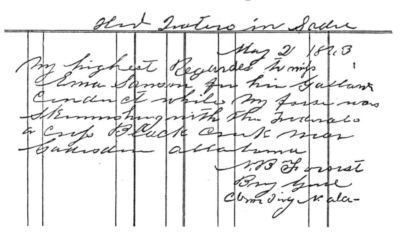

A copy of the actual note written by General Forrest to Emma Sansom. The handwriting is that of General Forrest.

Emma Sansom: Confederate Heroine

Emma held the note for a little while, then put it away and went back to the kitchen to be with her sister and Robert Turner.

"My sister and I sat up all night watching over the dead soldier, who had lost his life, fighting for our rights, in which we were overpowered but never conquered," Emma said.

"General Forrest and his men endeared themselves to us forever."

The grave of Robert Turner as it is today in the Sansom family cemetery in Gadsden. The cemetery lies in the median of U.S. Highway 431.

Epilogue

EMMA, JENNIE AND THEIR MOTHER buried Robert Turner in the Sansom family cemetery.

As far as anyone knows they never saw Nathan Bedford Forrest again.

But both Emma and Forrest carried memories of each other for the rest of their lives.

Forrest told others about the courage of young Emma and their moment together at Black Creek.

Emma named her first-born child after Forrest.

But the story of Streight's dash across Alabama and Forrest's chase does not end at Black Creek.

While Sergeant Williams was taking Emma home, Forrest was giving strict instructions to his men about crossing the creek.

Emma had shown Forrest the perfect place for his men to cross. It did not take long.

Forrest had given orders to his officers earlier

Emma Sansom: Confederate Heroine

An early artist's drawing of Forrest's men crossing the creek.

about how to get the ammunition across without getting it wet. When he arrived back from the Sansom farm, he was glad to see that his orders were being followed. The soldiers forded the creek on their horses, holding their ammunition high over their heads to keep it dry.

They strung ropes across the creek and pulled the cannons across with horses.

Once Forrest's army got across, they took off in a gallop after Streight.

Streight had no idea that Forrest would get across Black Creek so quickly. He took his men toward Gadsden, just a few miles away, in hopes that they could rest there and find food for themselves and their animals.

Margie Dover Ross

The Union soldiers were exhausted. Forrest never seemed to let up. The mules were dying and many of the Union wounded could not keep up. Streight left them on the side of the road.

The Union soldiers came storming into Gadsden about noon. A small quantity of food was quickly gathered from the Confederate commissaries, but it was not much. The Union soldiers began setting fire to parts of the town when they heard the familiar thunder of hooves not far behind them.

They did not bother to even look. They knew what was coming and fled as fast as they could.

The Confederates rode in and started putting out the fires that the Union soldiers had started.

Forrest still wasn't sure he could stop Streight in time, but he knew his chances were much better now that he was across Black Creek and nipping at Streight's heels. Forrest knew that the road to Rome crossed a bridge over the Oostanaula River. He sent a scout to Rome, ordering the people there to defend the Oostanaula River bridge or burn it to keep Streight out of the city.

Streight was closer to being finished than Forrest thought.

His men were exhausted. Streight marched them

Emma Sansom: Confederate Heroine

another 15 miles from Gadsden and knew they could go no more without rest. He came to a plantation where there were fields for the mules to graze, and where his men could eat and rest.

He had to stop, even if Forrest caught up.

It was late in the afternoon. Streight sent some men to feed the horses and mules, and had the others set up a battle line in case Forrest's army appeared

Not far away, Streight discovered a pine thicket and decided to hide his men there to ambush Forrest.

Forrest was too smart for the trick. He suspected that Streight was waiting in the thicket to ambush him. So, instead of taking his men through an open field beside the thicket where they would be easy targets, he told his men to ride their horses fast through the middle of the thicket. He also told them to shoot to the left and right as they rode through.

Not even aiming, the Rebels shot a lot of Union soldiers in the thicket. They rode so fast that Streight's men hardly had time to shoot back.

Streight pulled out quickly and began moving toward Rome again, trying his best to get away from Forrest.

Time was running out for Streight, and he knew it.

After failing to ambush Forrest at the pine thicket, he was desperate. His men were worn out from marching day and night for two days without rest. It did not matter. Streight told the men that they would march again for a third night.

He knew it was the only chance left.

They forged on, northeastward up the Coosa River valley.

As he had done before, Forrest told all but a few of his men to get a good night's sleep. The few he sent out to shoot at Streight's army all night long so they could not rest.

Those few good men caught up to Streight near the town of Centre, and made it hard on the Union soldiers for the rest of the night.

To make things worse, Streight's men had to take a long detour to find a way across the Coosa, and at one point found themselves lost in an area where logging roads wound in every direction.

By Sunday morning, May 3, Streight was less than 30 miles from Rome, but could not march another mile. The mules were collapsing and dying. The men could no longer march. It was near Cedar Bluff that they stopped.

That's where Forrest caught Streight, and tricked him into surrendering.

Forrest put part of his army in a semi-circle

around Streight's men, and Streight never could figure out how many men Forrest had.

Plus, the Union soldiers were so tired that they would fall asleep with their rifles cocked right on the battle line.

Forrest sent out a truce flag, and demanded Streight to surrender.

Streight wouldn't give up at first. He demanded to meet with Forrest.

And Forrest agreed.

"What is your proposition?" Streight asked.

"Immediate surrender," Forrest answered.

Streight told Forrest he wanted to talk with his officers about it first, and Forrest agreed but warned Streight not to take too much time.

"I have a column of fresh troops at hand, now nearer Rome than you are," Forrest told Streight. "You cannot cross the river in your front. I have men enough right here to run over you."

Forrest wasn't telling the truth, and Streight suspected as much, but he was not sure. So he told Forrest he wanted to see just how many Confederate soldiers there were.

Forrest was ready to trick Streight again. He had some men and a few cannons to circle round and round a nearby hill. It looked like there were lots of soldiers and cannons. But really it was just the same few going around and around.

Still, Streight was not convinced and told Forrest he would not quit.

Forrest never flinched.

Instead, he made his last bluff.

"Sound to mount," Forrest ordered his bugler.

Streight cried out. "I'll surrender!"

General Forrest breathed a sigh of relief. "Stack your arms right along there, Colonel, and march your men down that hollow," he told Streight.

When Streight saw how few men Forrest really had, he was furious. He told Forrest to give his soldiers their guns back and fight it out.

Forrest didn't agree. He just smiled and said, "Ah, Colonel, all is fair in love and war, you know."

Emma Sansom learned later that Forrest had caught Streight, and that the Union soldiers had surrendered. For the rest of her life, she was proud of the role she played in helping Forrest during that spring of 1863.

But did she ever know just how important her actions were that day?

That she gave Forrest the time he needed to catch the Union raiders even before they left Gadsden?

Emma Sansom: Confederate Heroine

Time for the battle-weary Confederates to rest?

Time for Forrest to outsmart Streight and force his surrender?

Time for the citizens of Rome, Georgia, to defend their city?

Time for the Atlanta to Chattanooga railroad to be saved?

Streight and what was left of his Army finally made it to Rome. They finally got to see the railroad there.

In fact they were loaded onto a train there. It carried them on the very tracks that they were supposed to destroy to Libby Prison in Richmond, Virginia.

The colonel was in prison about a year before he and some of his men escaped through a tunnel. He made his way to Washington, D.C., and later went back to combat.

Forrest fought to the end of the war and was one of the South's last generals to surrender. After the war he went back to his plantation, just south of Memphis. He suffered severe stomach ailments for several years and died on October 29, 1877, at the age of 56.

Margie Dover Ross

At Black Creek, Emma's brother Rufus came home after the war and married.

A soldier from the 10th Alabama Infantry named Christopher Ballard Johnson came back too. He fell in love with Emma Sansom and married her.

Their first baby was a girl. Emma named her Mattie Forrest Johnson. The child died soon after being born and is buried in the cemetery with Emma's father, Micajah Sansom, and Forrest's brave soldier, Robert Turner, who died in the fight at Black Creek.

Emma and her husband moved to a farm in Texas, a place called Little Mound in Upshur County, in the northeast part of the state. They had eight children—three girls and five boys.

Christopher Johnson died in 1884.

Emma died at age 52 on August 9, 1900.

She is buried in Little Mound Cemetery in Texas. On her tombstone, beneath her initials E.S.J. are these words: *Girl heroine who piloted General Forrest across Black Creek and enabled him to capture Colonel Streight.*

In 1907 the Gadsden Chapter of the United Daughters of the Confederacy erected a monument to Emma Sansom. She is depicted pointing the way to the Black Creek ford, with her sunbonnet in her hand. The monument is of white marble and life size and at the

Emma Sansom: Confederate Heroine

Sculpted from marble is the image of General Forrest and Emma Sansom, with Emma pointing the way to the Black Creek ford. This image is inset into the monument honoring Emma in Gadsden.

base of the statue is the image of Emma riding behind General Forrest on his horse.

Six months after the Black Creek incident, the Alabama Legislature honored Emma with a medal and a land grant. She wrote this letter of thanks to Governor John G. Shorter.

Respected Sir-I must acknowledge the receipt of your quite complimentary communication of Novemur

(sic) 27, 1863; and in doing so tender my gratitude for the more than expected respect shown me for having done my duty. At the time the duty was performed, it was a pleasure to be able to render some service to my country, and give aid to our noble cause. There are other duties, that would seem more becoming and adapted to my sex, but feeling it my high privilege upon such an occasion, I went forward, inspired by a sense of duty, and of the purest motives, willing to hazard women's timidity in giving aid to impede the onward march of the marauding foe... I must acknowledge my profound gratitude for the liberal donation by the State; and while I continue to live, I shall endeavor to render myself no more worthy of your high respect than heretofore. I have the satisfaction to be, very respectfully, your friend.
—*Emma Sansom*

The Sansom home does not exist today. Several school buildings occupy the land that once was the Sansom farm, and a four-lane federal highway, U.S. 431, runs through the land. The family cemetery is in the median of that highway. One of the schools is named General Forrest. The other is Emma Sansom High School.

Black Creek still tumbles off the falls, through the

Emma Sansom: Confederate Heroine

boulders to the foot of Lookout Mountain, and then runs dark and deep through the land that the Sansom's once farmed and where the soldiers once fought.

At the top of Lookout Mountain the City of Gadsden has built a nice park around Black Creek falls. They call it Noccalula Falls. The park offers camping, picnicking, walking trails where visitors can have a wonderful view of the waterfall and rising mist as it crashes into the rocky creek bottom.

Many people live in homes on top of the mountain today, but the creek still tumbles over boulders and under tall green trees down the side of the mountain.

When the creek reaches the valley, it slows quickly, just as it did in years past. In the place where Forrest and Streight fought, many of the trees are gone, replaced by houses, businesses and schools.

In other places along the creek, tall trees still hang over the water, dropping their leaves each fall into the deep pools and turning the water dark.

Margie Dover Ross

Emma Sansom

1847, August 16 Emma Sansom born to Micajah and Lamila Vann Sansom in Social Circle, Walton County, Georgia. She was their twelfth and last child.

1852 Moved with family to a farm near Black Creek in Cherokee County, Alabama (near Gadsden) This county is now called Etowah.

1859, December 24 Emma's father, Micajah Samson, dies.

1860, November 6 Abraham Lincoln is elected President.

1861 Rufus Sansom, Emma's brother, enters the Confederate army.

1861, January 11 Alabama votes to secede from

Emma Sansom: Confederate Heroine

the Union.

1861, February 4 Montgomery, Alabama becomes the capital of the Confederate States of America (CSA).

1861, April 12 Southern troops fire on Fort Sumter in Charleston, S.C.

1863, April 26 Streight pulls away from General Dodge and begins his raid across Alabama.

1863, April 28 Streight arrives in Moulton.

1863, April 29 Leaving from Courtland, Forrest begins his pursuit of Streight.

1863, May 1 Streight arrives in Blountsville.

1863, May 2 Emma rides on the back of General Forrest's horse to show him a ford where her cows crossed Black Creek, allowing him to quickly cross the stream and catch Streight.

1864 Alabama Legislature awards Emma Sansom a medal and promises her a section of land. The promise was not honored by the reconstruction Legislature because upon surrender of the Confederacy, all public lands belonged to the United States government.

1864, October 29 Emma marries Civil War veteran and member of the 10th Alabama Infantry, C.B. Johnson.

1876 Emma and C.B. Johnson move to Texas

1884 C.B. Johnson dies, leaving Emma with seven children.

1900, August 9 Emma Sansom Johnson dies one week short of her 53rd birthday.

1907 Monument erected in Emma Sansom's honor by the Gadsden Chapter of the United Daughters of the Confederacy.

Emma Sansom: Confederate Heroine

About the Author

Margie Dover Ross has been a library media specialist for students in grades K-8 for more than 14 years. She is the library media specialist at Shades Mountain Elementary School in Hoover, Alabama. Mrs. Ross holds an M.Ed. in Elementary Education with a concentration in library science from the University of Alabama in Birmingham. She is certified to teach K-8 and to be a library media specialist, K-12.

She is a past chair of the Children and School's Division of the Alabama Library Association, a member of the Alabama Geographic Alliance, Alabama Instructional Media Association and Delta Kappa Gamma Society International.

Margie Dover Ross

Emma Sansom: Confederate Heroine